332255

CAUSES, COURSE AND CONSEQUENCES

SIMON ADAMS

FRANKLIN WATTS
LONDON•SYDNEY

Designer Jason Billin
Editor Sarah Ridley
Art Director Jonathan Hair
Editor-in-Chief John C. Miles
Picture research Diana Morris
Map artwork Ian Thompson

© 2005 Franklin Watts

First published in 2005
by Franklin Watts
96 Leonard Street
London
EC2A 4XD

Franklin Watts Australia
Level 17/207 Kent Street
Sydney NSW 2000

ISBN 0 7496 6356 1

A CIP catalogue record for this book is
available from the British Library.

Printed in China

Dewey number: 940.53

Picture credits
Cody Images: cover, 5, 8, 9, 11,
   12, 16,18, 20, 23, 25, 30, 31, 32
Peter Newark's Pictures: 15
Popperfoto: 6, 27

*Every attempt has been made to clear
copyright. Should there be any
inadvertent omission please apply to the
publisher for rectification.*

Note to parents and teachers:
Every effort has been made by the Publishers
to ensure that the websites in this book are
suitable for children, that they are of the
highest educational value, and that they
contain no inappropriate or offensive
material. However, because of the nature of
the Internet, it is impossible to guarantee
that the contents of these sites will not be
altered. We strongly advise that Internet
access is supervised by a responsible adult.

CONTENTS

Introduction

Between 1939 and 1945, the countries of the world fought the most violent and devastating war in the whole of history. Millions of soldiers and civilians lost their lives. Whole countries were destroyed and towns and cities ruined. This book looks at the history of this war, why it started, what happened, and what effects it had.

The World at War

World War Two was truly global in scale. Most European, North African and south-east Asian countries as well as the USA and Canada were directly involved in the fighting while many others, such as those in Latin America, were caught up in events as war raged. Some of the European nations, notably Britain, France and Italy, had empires in Africa, Asia and Australasia, whose peoples joined their armies.

By 1945 only nine nations remained out of the war: Portugal and Spain (and their African colonies), Ireland, Sweden and Switzerland in Europe, and Afghanistan, Nepal, Mongolia and Yemen in Asia. Every other European and Asian nation, and every American, Australasian and African nation was at war.

A World War

Although the war started in Europe, it soon spread to Africa, Asia, Australasia and the Americas, making it a truly world war. Almost every country in the world fought in the war, or was affected by it. We call it World War Two, or the Second World War, to separate it from World War One (1914-18).

A Human War

Everybody's lives were affected. Millions of people were called up to fight in the armed services. Millions more worked in factories and shipyards, producing weapons and other war supplies. Many lost their lives in the fighting, while a whole generation of young men and women lost six years of their youth to the war.

For those not directly involved in the fighting, life was equally harsh. Food was rationed, or in short supply, and there were few things to buy in the shops. Many people lived in fear of enemy air raids which claimed thousands of lives and homes. Large numbers of people were evacuated from cities to save them from enemy attacks. Across Europe and Asia, millions of people lived under enemy occupation. They were often forced to work or fight for the enemy against their own country or people. Many died when they were caught up in the fighting.

New Weapons

The war saw the development of many deadly new weapons, such as the armed rocket and the hugely powerful atomic bomb. Tanks, submarines, warships, fighter planes and bombers all became much more powerful, while many new types of gun and artillery equipment came into use.

A Total War

In order to win the war, the main countries involved – Germany, Japan, Russia, Britain, the USA and their many allies – devoted all their military, economic, industrial, physical and human strength to win the war. The war affected every part of society and everybody within it. That is why World War Two is often called a "total war".

A gun crew in action at night in North Africa, 1942.

> **66 This war is a new kind of war. It is warfare in terms of every continent, every island, every sea, every air lane in the world. 99**
>
> *President Franklin D Roosevelt, wartime president of the USA, February 1942*

The World After World War One

World War Two was the direct result of World War One, which saw the defeat of Germany and her allies by Britain, France and the USA in 1918. Although it was not clear at the time, the peace treaties agreed after World War One would keep the peace between nations for only twenty years.

Fascism and Nazism

Fascism was an extreme political movement developed by Benito Mussolini (1883-1945) in Italy. Fascists believed in nationalism, extreme loyalty to their country, and aimed to unite a country's people into a disciplined force under an all-powerful leader. Nazism was an even more extreme version of fascism and was developed by Adolf Hitler (1889-1945) in Germany. Nazis were strongly anti-Semitic and believed that the Germans were a "master race" who should dominate the world. Between 1922 and 1945, fascism flourished in Italy, Spain, Austria, Croatia and across much of Eastern Europe, while Nazis took control in Germany after 1933. The Japanese government, although fascist in many ways, was increasingly run as a military dictatorship.

Germany

After its defeat, Germany was forced to sign humiliating peace terms at Versailles in France in 1919. It lost much of its land, including overseas colonies, was forbidden to form a large army and had to pay huge amounts of money to the victors. A republic was established, but it was weak and few people had confidence in it.

Many Germans did not accept their country's defeat in 1918 and believed their country had been betrayed by communists, Jews and other supposed enemies of the state. They began to listen to the views of extreme political parties, notably the National Socialist (Nazi) Party led by Adolf Hitler. The Nazis remained a small force in German politics until the German economy collapsed during the

A mobile soup kitchen hands out meals to the hungry in 1920s Germany.

GERMANY BEFORE AND AFTER WORLD WAR ONE

Frontier of German
Empire, 1914

Germany,
1919

worldwide economic slump of 1929. By 1932 the
Nazis were the biggest political party in the
German Reichstag, or parliament.

Italy and Japan

Two other countries emerged dissatisfied from
World War One. Although both Italy and Japan
had been on the winning side, they did not feel
they had been rewarded enough. In Italy, the
government after the war was weak and divided.
Many people turned to Benito Mussolini's extreme
Fascist Party which took power in 1922 and soon
banned all other political parties. Mussolini built
up Italian military strength and looked to expand
Italy's small overseas empire.

Like Italy, Japan had only emerged as a major
world nation at the end of the previous century.
Japanese nationalists – who disliked their country's
close ties with the USA and other western nations
– wanted to establish a major regional empire in
eastern Asia. When the Japanese economy
collapsed during the slump of 1929, nationalists in
the armed services seized their chance. They
gradually took control of the government and
ignored parliament. In 1931 Japanese troops
seized control of the vast northern Chinese
province of Manchuria. A new Japanese military
empire was about to be created.

1918-1931

November 1918 World War One ends with
defeat of Germany and her allies by
Britain, France, the USA and their allies.

March 1919 Benito Mussolini forms *Fasci
d'Italiani di Combattimento* (the Italian
Fascist Party).

June 1919 Treaty of Versailles punishes
Germany for its role in World War One.

July 1919 German republic established in
Weimar.

September 1919 Adolf Hitler joins German
Worker's Party, later known as the
National Socialist (Nazi) Party.

October 1922 Fascist Party members stage
"March on Rome" to seize power;
Italian king invites Mussolini to form
new government.

September 1923 Hyper-inflation – a rapid
and severe fall in the value of money –
wipes out people's savings in Germany.

July 1925 Hitler publishes *Mein Kampf*
(*My Struggle*) his personal declaration of
political beliefs.

October 1929 New York Stock Exchange in
Wall Street crashes, leading to a
worldwide economic slump by 1933.

September 1931 Japanese forces seize
Manchuria, part of northern China.

**❝The First [World] War
explains the second and,
in fact, caused it.
...Germany fought in the
Second War to reverse the
verdict of the first and to
destroy the settlement
that followed it.❞**

*AJP Taylor, British historian and author of
The Origins of the Second World War
(1961)*

The Approach to War

In January 1933 Adolf Hitler became chancellor (prime minister) of an economically and politically weak Germany. Six years later, Germany dominated Europe and the world stood on the brink of a new world war.

The British prime minister, Neville Chamberlain, returns from Munich, Germany, in 1938 with the agreement that provided "peace for our time" (see below).

The Munich Crisis

After the union with Austria in March 1938, Hitler turned his attention to Czechoslovakia. He threatened to invade unless the Sudetenland border region was united with Germany. At a conference in Munich in September, the leaders of Britain, France and Italy agreed to German demands; the Czechs were not consulted. The British prime minister, Neville Chamberlain, said that the Munich Agreement provided "peace for our time". However, in March 1939 German troops marched into western Czechoslovakia.

Hitler leads Germany

The worldwide economic slump of 1929 wrecked the German economy. By 1932 two out of every five Germans were out of work. On 30 January 1933, President Hindenburg asked Hitler to form a new government. Hitler banned all opposition parties, took dictatorial powers and, in August 1934, became "*Führer* (leader) of the German *Reich* (empire)" and supreme commander of the armed forces.

Hitler rapidly built up the German forces and in 1936 reoccupied the demilitarised Rhineland between Germany and France, actions forbidden by the Treaty of Versailles. He also built up German industry and got the unemployed back into work.

International Expansion

Italy too began to expand its territory, occupying the east African nation of Abyssinia (Ethiopia) by 1936 and the southern European state of Albania in April 1939. Japan continued to seize territory in China, invading the north and centre of the country in July 1937. In 1938 Japan announced a "New Order" in eastern Asia – dominated economically and militarily by Japan.

At first, Germany and Italy acted independently, but in October 1936 they reached an agreement known as the Rome-Berlin Axis; during World War Two, Germany and its allies would be known as the Axis powers. A month later, Germany signed a similar agreement with Japan known as the Anti-Comintern Pact, directed against their mutual enemy, the USSR or Soviet Russia. Italy joined this alliance the following year.

The League of Nations, set up by the Treaty of Versailles in 1919, proved powerless to prevent Axis aggression. Germany and Japan had left the League in 1933, followed by Italy in 1937. By 1939 the three were ready to try to dominate the world.

Nazi Germany relied on elaborate ceremonies to reinforce power. This is the Nuremburg Rally of 1933.

1933-1939

30 January 1933 President Hindenburg asks Adolf Hitler to form a government.

February 1933 Reichstag, or parliament building, catches fire; Hitler uses this as an excuse to ban opposition parties.

March 1933 Enabling Act gives Hitler dictatorial powers.

1 August 1934 President Hindenburg dies; Hitler becomes Führer.

October 1935-August 1936 Italy invades and occupies Abyssinia.

March 1936 German troops occupy demilitarised Rhineland.

October 1936 Rome-Berlin Axis: Italy and Germany become allies.

November 1936 German-Japanese Anti-Comintern Pact against USSR.

July 1937 Japan invades all of China.

March 1938 *Anschluss,* or union, between Austria and Germany.

September 1938 Munich Agreement.

March 1939 Germany occupies western Czechoslovakia.

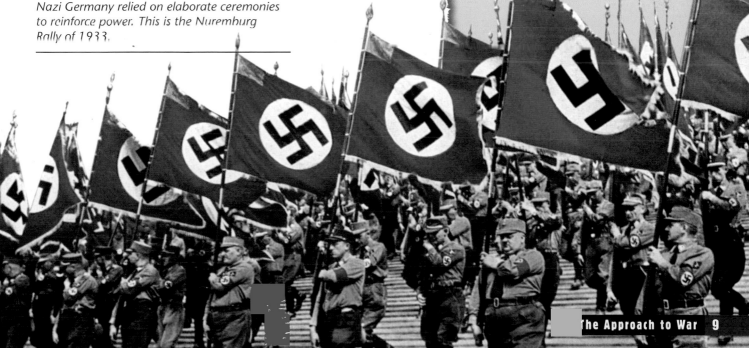

1939

In 1939 the world stood on the brink of war. Germany had acquired Austria and Czechoslovakia and now turned its attention towards Poland. But first Germany had to reach a deal with the one country that could stand in its way, the USSR and its leader, Josef Stalin.

The Nazi-Soviet Pact

The non-aggression pact signed on 23 August 1939 between the German foreign minister, Ribbentrop, and his Soviet counterpart, Molotov, guaranteed that both countries would remain neutral if the other was at war. Secret clauses agreed the division of Poland between the two nations, and allowed Russia to occupy Finland, the Baltic states of Estonia, Latvia and (by a later agreement) Lithuania and eastern Romania.

At much the same time, Russia agreed a peace treaty with Japan to end conflicts along their disputed border in Manchuria. Both Germany and Japan could now operate without fear of Russian intervention.

The Threat to Poland

After the occupation of Czechoslovakia, Germany began to demand the city of Danzig on the Baltic Sea. Danzig was a neutral city whose independence was guaranteed by the League of Nations. Germany also wanted access to its province of East Prussia through the corridor of land that linked Poland to the Baltic. When Poland refused both demands, Hitler instructed his armed forces to prepare to invade. He believed that Britain and France were too weak to oppose him and would not go to war over Poland.

The German invasion of Czechoslovakia, however, broke the Munich Agreement that was meant to guarantee peace. Britain and France now realised that there was no point trying to negotiate with Hitler to prevent war. They therefore promised to support Poland if Germany invaded. They later extended this promise to Greece and Romania.

The Nazi-Soviet Pact

By this time, the USSR was seriously alarmed by German expansion in Central Europe. Since 1917, Soviet Russia had been the world's only communist state; it had few friends abroad. Hitler and the Nazis were strongly anti-communist, so the USSR feared that Germany might attack it too. In April 1939 it proposed an alliance with Britain and France to stop Hitler. However, the two nations were slow to respond so it signed a non-aggression pact with Nazi Germany on 23 August 1939 (see box). Germany became free to attack Poland without Russian intervention.

The Start of War

On 1 September, Germany invaded Poland. When it refused to withdraw, Britain, France and their vast overseas empires (known as the "Allies" because they were allied against Axis aggression) declared war. World War Two had begun.

Germany's campaign against Poland consisted of a rapid tank and armoured vehicle *blitzkrieg* (lightning war) supported by a heavy air bombardment that overwhelmed the Polish army. Moreover, on 17 September Russian forces invaded from the east, dividing the country in two.

1 September 1939: German troops march into Poland.

1939

March Germany occupies western Czechoslovakia: eastern half becomes German-allied state of Slovakia.

March Germany seizes Baltic port of Memel from Lithuania and demands free city of Danzig and corridor of land linking Poland to the Baltic Sea; Poland refuses.

March Britain and France offer to support Poland if it is invaded by Germany.

April USSR proposes an alliance with Britain and France to stop Germany.

August Germany signs non-aggression pact with USSR.

1 September Germany occupies Poland.

3 September Britain and France declare war on Germany, joined by Australia, New Zealand and later Canada; World War Two begins.

15 September Japan signs peace agreement with USSR.

17 September Soviet forces occupy eastern Poland.

1940

After the defeat of Poland in September 1939, a "phoney war" began in Europe. Both sides prepared for war, but no fighting occurred. The exception was Finland, which was at war with Russia until March 1940. This period of inactivity came to an abrupt end the following month.

The Fall of France

German troops first entered France on 13 May and reached Paris a month later on 14 June. A week later they had conquered all but the south of the country. The French government collapsed in the face of this advance and appointed Marshal Pétain, hero of the defence of Verdun during World War One, to run the country. He agreed an armistice (truce) with Germany. The Germans were to control the north and west of the country, while a pro-German government led by Pétain governed the south from the town of Vichy. Some Frenchmen decided to fight on: in London, General Charles de Gaulle established the Free French movement to fight for the liberation of France from the Germans.

Norway

In early 1940, both sides turned their attention to Norway. The Allies wanted to stop the Germans shipping much-needed iron ore out of neighbouring Sweden through Norwegian ports. The Germans wanted to use it as a naval base to attack convoys of merchant ships bringing supplies to Britain from North America. In April 1940 the Germans successfully invaded Denmark and then Norway.

The Allied defeat in Norway led to the resignation of Neville Chamberlain as British prime minister and his replacement by Winston Churchill, who formed a coalition government of all political parties.

Adolf Hitler poses in front of the Eiffel Tower in Paris, June 1940.

Western Europe

The Germans then invaded Western Europe. Holland, Belgium and Luxembourg, overwhelmed, surrendered within days. As the Germans pushed westwards into France, they surrounded thousands of Allied troops at Dunkirk, who were evacuated by sea using a fleet of small ships sent across the Channel from England. In June, the Germans entered Paris and the French surrendered. Britain and its empire now stood alone.

The Battle of Britain

Hitler now turned his attention to Operation Sea Lion – the planned invasion of Britain. German bombers attacked military targets but were beaten off by the Royal Air Force (RAF) during the Battle of Britain. As a result, Operation Sea Lion was postponed. German bombers then targeted British cities in "the Blitz". Thousands were killed or made homeless. Meanwhile, in the Battle of the Atlantic, German U-boats attacked British and allied shipping from bases in France, sinking hundreds of ships and preventing supplies reaching Britain.

Italy enters the War

In June 1940 Italy had entered the war on the German side and invaded France. It then attacked Egypt and British colonies in East Africa, extending the war onto the African continent. After early successes, it suffered huge losses. In October 1940, Italian troops invaded Greece from Albania, but they too were repelled. It soon became clear that Germany would have to help its Italian ally.

1940

12 March Treaty of Moscow ends "Winter War" between Russia and Finland; Finns lose border regions to USSR.

9 April Germans occupy Denmark and invade Norway.

14 April Allied troops land in Norway but fail to prevent German occupation.

10 May Chamberlain resigns as British prime minister; Winston Churchill takes over; Germany occupies Holland, Belgium, Luxembourg and France.

26 May-4 June Evacuation of Allied troops from Dunkirk.

10 June Italy enters war on German side and occupies southern France.

14 June Germans enter Paris.

18 June In London, General de Gaulle rallies French resistance behind the Free French movement.

18 June Russia occupies three Baltic states and eastern Romania.

22 June French leader Marshal Pétain signs armistice with Germany.

30 June German forces land in the Channel Islands, the only part of the United Kingdom occupied during the war.

4 July Italians attack British colonies in East Africa.

10 July-12 October Battle of Britain fought in skies over southern England; German *Luftwaffe* (air force) fails to overcome British Royal Air Force.

7 September German bombers begin "the Blitz" against British cities.

12 September Italians invade Egypt from Libya in order to seize the Suez Canal.

27 September Germany, Italy and Japan sign Tripartite Pact.

12 October Hitler postpones Operation Sea Lion, ending his attempt to invade Britain.

20 October Hungary joins Tripartite Pact, followed by Romania and Bulgaria.

28 October Italy occupies Greece.

1941

With the collapse of France in June 1940, Britain and its empire stood alone against Germany and Italy. By the end of 1941, that situation had completely changed. The entry of first the USSR and then the USA into the war turned the conflict into a truly global affair and, in the end, decided its outcome.

Why was the USSR caught by surprise?

One of the biggest puzzles of the war is why the USSR was caught by surprise by the massive German invasion of 22 June 1941. The Russians had received warning of the invasion from the British and from their own spies, while the German military build-up in Poland could not easily be hidden. Yet the USSR took no steps to prepare itself.

One theory is that the Red Army was not yet ready for war, so the Soviet leader Stalin did not want to do anything that might provoke Hitler to invade. Another, less likely theory is that Stalin was preparing his own attack on Germany at some point. Either way, the Soviet failure was to prove very costly in both lives and equipment.

Africa

After early Italian successes, the British expelled the Italians from East Africa and inflicted huge losses in Libya. In response, Hitler sent Erwin Rommel, one of his leading generals, to North Africa to support the Italians. Rommel soon pushed the British troops back towards Egypt. The battle for North Africa then swung back and forth without a major victory on either side.

The Balkans

Hitler took the decision to invade the USSR in late 1940. He needed support from the Balkan countries and access to Romania's oilfields to achieve success. Hungary, Bulgaria and Romania all agreed to join the Tripartite Pact (Germany, Italy, Japan), but Yugoslavia refused. So, German armies invaded Yugoslavia. They also invaded Greece to support the Italians.

Operation Barbarossa

On 22 June 1941, Germany deployed 3.6 million men, 3,600 tanks and 2,700 aircraft in a surprise attack against the USSR. Within days, the Red Air Force had been almost totally destroyed and 600,000 troops – one-third of the Soviet Red Army – had been killed or captured. By the end of the year, German troops were within sight of Moscow before the harsh winter weather prevented further advances.

US battleships ablaze and sinking as Japanese forces attack Pearl Harbor, 7 December 1941.

Pearl Harbor

In the Far East, Japan had continued to advance into China and occupied military bases in French Indo-China. In response, Britain, the USA and the Dutch East Indies stopped all trade with Japan, cutting off almost all its oil imports. Faced with this threat to its supplies, Japanese planes bombed the US Pacific Fleet at Pearl Harbor in Hawaii. This brought the USA into the war on the side of Britain and the USSR, against the Axis powers.

> **Yesterday, December 7, 1941 ... the United States of America was suddenly and deliberately attacked by naval and air forces of the Empire of Japan.**

President Franklin D Roosevelt of the USA declaring war on Japan, 8 December 1941

1941

12 February General Rommel arrives in North Africa to support Italian forces.

4 March British troops land in Greece to support the fight against Italy.

25 March Yugoslavia joins Tripartite Pact but withdraws two days later after its government is overthrown.

5 April Germany invades Yugoslavia and Greece.

11 April Rommel surrounds and besieges Tobruk in Libya.

12 April Yugoslavia surrenders, followed by Greece on 21 April.

13 April USSR signs neutrality pact with Japan, releasing troops from Siberia to defend country against possible German invasion.

16 May Italian troops in Eritrea, Ethiopia and Somaliland surrender to the British; Haile Selassie restored to throne of Abyssinia (Ethiopia) from which he had been expelled in 1936.

31 May British forces leave Crete (Greece), their last foothold in Europe.

22 June In Operation Barbarossa, Germany and its allies invade the USSR, which now enters war on Allied side with Britain.

28 July Japanese occupy bases in Indo-China.

5 August USA, UK and the Netherlands stop all trade with Japan.

15 September Germans begin 900-day siege of Leningrad.

23 November Germans within 56 kilometres of Moscow.

3 December Allies relieve Tobruk from German siege.

7 December Japanese forces attack US Pacific Fleet at Pearl Harbor; USA enters war against the Axis powers the next day.

December Japanese attack Thailand, Malaya, the Philippines and Borneo, capturing British colony of Hong Kong on Christmas Day.

1942

At the start of the year, Germany was triumphant in Russia while Japan was sweeping all before it in the Far East. Three decisive battles during the year, however, changed the course of the war and gave the advantage to the Allies.

US aircraft carriers sail into battle at Midway, June 1942.

Bombing the Enemy

In the first three years of the war, aerial bombing by both German and British planes was mainly directed at specific military and economic targets, such as docks or airports, although civilians living nearby were often killed. In May 1942 this strategy changed when Britain's RAF Bomber Command attacked the German city of Cologne in the first 1,000-bomber raid. This new strategy of "area bombing" aimed to destroy everything in the area. Both sides believed that a sustained bombing campaign would undermine the morale of the civilian population and force the enemy to make peace, but it failed to have that effect.

The Far East

In the early months of the year, the Japanese overran south-east Asia, capturing Burma, Malaya, Singapore, the Dutch East Indies, and the Philippines. In the Pacific, they captured island after island, massively extending their empire (see map on page 29). In April-May, a long-range naval battle took place north-east of Australia between the US and Japanese fleets, the first aircraft-carrier battle in history. US aeroplanes prevented a Japanese assault on Port Moresby, capital of Papua, within easy distance of northern Australia. A far greater success came at Midway Island in June. Here the Japanese attempt to capture the US military airbase was stopped and its fleet largely destroyed; this was the first major Allied victory of the war. From then on, the Japanese were on the defensive in the Pacific.

North Africa

In June, General Rommel managed at last to capture Tobruk for the Germans and then advance into Egypt. His plan was to throw the British out of Egypt and capture the Suez Canal, cutting a vital supply route to and from India and the Far East. The decisive battle took place in October at El Alamein, just to the west of Alexandria and the Nile Delta. Here British General Bernard Montgomery and his 8th Army – the "Desert Rats" – achieved the first British battle victory of the war. In early November, US and British troops landed in Morocco and Algeria and advanced east, threatening the Germans from the rear and securing the North African coastline for the Allies.

Stalingrad

The third major battle took place at Stalingrad on the River Volga in southern Russia. The German 6th Army attacked the city in August and eventually forced its Russian defenders into a thin line along the Volga. However, Soviet forces encircled the Germans from behind in November and besieged them. Fighting continued with great loss of life on both sides until the Germans surrendered in February 1943. From then on, the Germans were on the defensive throughout Russia.

1942

11 January Japanese invade Dutch East Indies and British colony of Burma.

20 January At the Wannsee Conference, leading Nazis agree the "Final Solution of the Jewish Question", the mass murder of 6 million Jews at concentration and death camps throughout occupied Europe.

31 January Japanese complete conquest of Malaya.

15 February British surrender in Singapore.

28 April-8 May Battle of Coral Sea halts Japanese advance in south-west Pacific.

7 May Japanese conquer Philippines.

30 May First Allied 1,000-bomber raid devastates German city of Cologne.

4-6 June US fleet stops Japanese invasion of Midway Island in the Pacific.

21 June Tobruk finally falls to the Germans.

19 August German 6th Army begins attack on Stalingrad.

23 October-4 November Rommel defeated at El Alamein.

25-27 October Major US naval victory against the Japanese at Battle of Santa Cruz in the Solomon Islands as fight continues for strategic island of Guadalcanal.

8 November Operation Torch – US and British troops land in north-west Africa.

11 November German troops occupy Vichy France and end its independence.

23 November Red Army surrounds German 6th Army at Stalingrad.

"Ring out the bells!"

General Alexander, overall commander of the British Middle East forces, in message to Churchill after the victory at El Alamein, 6 November 1942

1943

In 1943 the tide of war turned decisively in favour of the Allies, although there were still many battles to fight. A "second front" opened up in Europe, and one of Germany's allies was removed from the war.

The Battle of Kursk

In summer 1943, the biggest tank battle in history took place near Kursk in central Russia. Soviet successes and German counter-attacks had left a huge bulge in the front line. The Germans moved to regain their positions but were met with a massive Soviet response. More than 6,000 tanks and two million men took part in the battle, which ended in Soviet victory.

North Africa

In January, the British captured the Libyan capital of Tripoli and advanced into Tunisia. Despite a desperate German fightback, Rommel was unable to hold off the joint British and American attack and left Tunisia in March. By May the Allies had captured Tunis, capital of Tunisia, and both the German and Italian armies surrendered. The Allies had won the battle for North Africa and could now turn their attention towards Europe.

The Invasion of Italy

Ever since the USA had entered the war in December 1941, the Soviets had urged their western allies to

Stalingrad was reduced almost to ruins by the fighting for control of the city.

open a "second front" in Europe to take the pressure off the Red Army in the east. With North Africa in Allied hands, it was now possible to cross the Mediterranean in safety. So on 9 July Allied troops landed in Sicily to begin the invasion of Italy. Mussolini was overthrown and in September, an armistice (truce) was signed with the new Italian government. Allied troops then landed in southern Italy but the Germans quickly occupied Rome, where they freed Mussolini from gaol. For the next 18 months, Allied troops had to fight their way up the Italian peninsula against fierce German resistance.

The Eastern Front

After the catastrophic German defeat at Stalingrad, the Soviet Red Army took the offensive. The Germans were steadily pushed out of Ukraine and the Caucasus in the south of the country and away from Moscow in the centre. After the massive tank battle at Kursk (see box), the Red Army recaptured Kharkov and then Kiev, before crossing the River Dnieper to establish a new front line in western Ukraine.

The Pacific

During 1943, Japan and the USA strengthened their forces as they prepared for the battles ahead. The Japanese had established a heavily fortified frontier of islands thousands of kilometres from their homeland, but were defeated at both Guadalcanal and New Guinea. The Americans had the advantage of a bigger navy as well as air superiority. They therefore began to pick off each Japanese-held island one by one, hopping over heavily fortified islands in a cartwheel action that slowly took them closer to Japan itself.

1943

14-24 January At a conference in Casablanca with Prime Minister Churchill, President Roosevelt demands the "unconditional surrender" of Germany, Italy and Japan.

28 January British capture Tripoli, capital of Libya.

2 February Germans surrender at Stalingrad.

8 February Japanese finally evacuate Guadalcanal in the Solomon Islands.

9 February Japanese defeated in eastern New Guinea.

6 March Rommel leaves Tunisia.

19 April-16 May Jewish uprising in Warsaw ghetto crushed by Germans.

12-13 May German and Italian armies surrender in Tunisia.

30 June US begins Operation Cartwheel to clear Japanese off Solomon Islands.

4-15 July Major tank battle at Kursk in central Russia.

9 July Allied airborne troops land on Sicily.

25 July Mussolini overthrown in Italy.

23 August Red Army finally recaptures Kharkov in northern Ukraine.

3 September Armistice signed between Italy and Allies; Allied troops land in southern Italy.

8 September Italy surrenders.

10 September Germans occupy Rome; Mussolini is rescued by Germans and sets up new fascist government.

4 October French island of Corsica liberated by Allies.

6 November Red Army recaptures Ukrainian capital of Kiev and crosses the River Dnieper.

28 Nov–1 Dec The "Big Three" – Churchill, Roosevelt, Stalin – meet for first time in Teheran, Iran, to plan war strategy.

1944

As the Red Army continued to push westwards, driving the Germans out of Russia and Ukraine, a new front was opened up in France. On D-Day, thousands of Allied troops landed on the beaches of Normandy, France, in the biggest seaborne invasion ever launched.

D-Day

The decision to invade France through Normandy, rather than at the closer and more likely landing point in the Pas de Calais, was taken in March 1943. The Allies managed to keep this decision secret until D-Day itself. Hitler was therefore forced to spread his defensive forces along all possible invasion sites, allowing the Allies to land without overwhelming opposition.

After the inital landings, two floating Mulberry harbours were towed across the Channel. One broke up in heavy storms, but the other was used to unload up to 11,000 tons of equipment each day. On 12 August, an oil pipeline from England under the sea to Cherbourg came into use, providing a constant supply of fuel for armoured vehicles and trucks.

D-Day

Operation Overlord – the invasion of France – required immense planning: more than 6,500 naval and transport craft in 75 convoys, supported by 12,000 aircraft, were assembled in southern English ports to ferry the 150,000-strong American, British and Canadian invasion force across the English Channel on the night of 5-6 June. The troops landed on five beaches and then secured a foothold in northern Normandy.

The D-Day landings: troops wade ashore in Normandy on 6 June 1944.

The Liberation of France

The breakout from Normandy came on 25 July, when US troops broke through the German lines. French troops liberated Paris on 25 August while the main Allied armies sped eastwards towards the German frontier. Meanwhile, Allied troops had landed in southern France and were advancing northwards. By the end of the year, France, Belgium and southern Holland were liberated from German control.

The Battle of the Bulge

On 16 December, German troops suddenly attacked westwards, catching the Allies by surprise and creating a bulge in the front line. The advance was halted within 10 days and then reversed. It was the last big German offensive in Western Europe. Once it was defeated, the Allies could advance into Germany.

The Eastern Front

The Red Army continued to expel the Germans, first from the Crimea and Ukraine, and then from central Russia and the Baltic states. In July they crossed the Polish frontier. In the Balkans, the Red Army liberated Romania, Bulgaria and all but the north of Yugoslavia. By the end of the year, the Red Army was ready for a final assault on Germany.

The Pacific

In the Pacific, US troops moved steadily westwards towards Japan, defeating a massive Japanese fleet in the Philippines Sea during June. After landing in the Philippines in October, the US fleet defeated the Japanese navy at Leyte Gulf. US bombers were now within striking distance of Japan itself.

1944

22 January-3 March Allies establish a beachhead at Anzio, south of Rome.

24 January-18 May Allies capture Monte Cassino in central Italy after a lengthy and bloody battle.

27 January German siege of Leningrad lifted after 900 days.

31 January US troops capture Marshall Islands from Japan.

4 June Allies enter Rome.

6 June D-Day Allied landings on the beaches of Normandy.

10 June Normandy beachheads joined together to create single Allied foothold in France.

15 June-24 July US troops occupy Mariana Islands.

19-20 June Massive Japanese naval losses during Battle of Philippines Sea.

17 July Red Army crosses frontier into Poland.

25 July Operation Cobra – US troops break out of Normandy into central France.

15 August Operation Anvil – Allied troops land in southern France.

25 August French troops liberate Paris.

31 August Red Army enters Bucharest, the Romanian capital, and then moves into Bulgaria.

14 September Allied troops liberate Belgium and reach German and Dutch frontiers.

4 October British troops land in Greece and liberate Athens.

17 October US troops invade Philippines.

20 October Yugoslav capital, Belgrade, liberated by partisans and the Red Army.

22-27 October Massive Japanese naval defeat in Leyte Gulf in the Philippines.

16-26 December Germans launch massive attack westwards into Belgium, catching Allies by surprise.

1945

At the start of 1945, the Allies stood either side of Germany, ready to advance towards the German capital, Berlin, and bring the Nazi regime to an end. But the war against Japan looked likely to continue for two or more years, with considerable loss of life, as the Japanese put up massive resistance.

The Atomic Bombs

The physics required to make an atomic bomb had been discovered by two German scientists in 1938. They split a uranium atom and caused a chain reaction of massive power. After the USA entered the war, a team of atomic scientists worked to turn this discovery into a weapon.

The Manhattan Project, as it was called, was led by Robert Oppenheimer and was based at Los Alamos in New Mexico. By July 1945, the team had produced three bombs. The first was tested in the New Mexico desert on 16 July, the second was dropped on the Japanese city of Hiroshima on 6 August, the third on Nagasaki three days later. The two bombs killed 220,000 Japanese citizens, with probably the same number dying later of radiation sickness.

The Western Front

Once the German offensive into Belgium was crushed, the Allies could cross the Rhine into Germany itself. The bridge at Remagen, north of Koblenz, was undamaged and undefended, allowing the Allies to flood into central Germany. Most German troops were fighting the Red Army in the east, so the western Allies made huge advances, meeting the Red Army coming in the other direction on the River Elbe in late April.

The Eastern Front

By comparison, the Red Army advance was far slower and far more costly. Warsaw was taken in January, but Budapest, the Hungarian capital, only fell after a lengthy siege in February. By then, the Red Army had crossed the River Oder and was only 64 kilometres from Berlin. Hitler put every effort into the defence of Berlin, but by 25 April the Red Army surrounded the city and broke into the centre. On 30 April, two Russian soldiers raised the Soviet flag over the Reichstag in Berlin. By then, Hitler had committed suicide and the Reich lay in ruins.

As German forces surrendered throughout Europe, a complete surrender was agreed on 7 May. The next day, the Allies celebrated VE (Victory in Europe) Day. The war in the west was finally over.

The atomic bombs dropped on Hiroshima and Nagasaki unleashed the massive destructive potential of the atom.

The War against Japan

In the Far East, the main task of the US forces was to acquire air bases from which to attack Japan. In January and February they captured the Philippine island of Luzon, but 146,000 US troops died in the process. The next targets were Iwo Jima and Okinawa. The Japanese resisted fiercely; they seemed set to fight to the death.

During the war, scientists had developed the devastating atomic bomb (see box). The new US president, Harry Truman, took the decision to drop two atomic bombs on the Japanese cities of Hiroshima and Nagasaki. After the declaration of war by the USSR on 8 August, Japan finally surrendered. On 15 August, VJ (Victory against Japan) Day was celebrated. The war against Japan was over. World War Two had come to an end.

1945

17 January Red Army enters Warsaw.

25 January US troops attack main Philippine island of Luzon.

26 January Red Army liberates Auschwitz concentration camp; the horrors of the Holocaust begin to be exposed to the world.

3 February Red Army crosses River Oder, just kilometres from Berlin.

11 February Red Army takes Budapest after a six-week siege.

13-14 February 100,000 civilians die when British and US planes bomb Dresden, in Germany, causing a massive firestorm.

7 March Allies cross undefended bridge at Remagen over the River Rhine.

26 March US troops capture island of Iwo Jima after a five-week campaign.

5 April After a harsh winter, Allies begin new offensive in Italy.

12 April President Roosevelt of the US dies and is succeeded by Harry Truman.

25 April Red Army surrounds Berlin; US and Soviet troops first make contact near Torgau on the River Elbe.

28 April Mussolini caught and killed by Italian partisans.

30 April Hitler commits suicide in his bunker in Berlin.

2 May Armistice in Italy.

7 May German troops agree unconditional surrender.

8 May VE Day celebrated throughout Europe.

30 June US troops finally take Okinawa.

6 August Atomic bomb dropped on Hiroshima, with a second on Nagasaki on 9 August.

8 August USSR declares war on Japan and invades Manchuria.

14 August Japan agrees to surrender.

15 August VJ Day celebrated.

The Cost of the War

The final defeat of Germany and then Japan brought peace for the first time in six years. Yet the world was in turmoil, with millions dead, millions more injured or homeless, and entire countries ruined. Making the peace was going to be as difficult as fighting the war.

The Marshall Plan

Aid was accepted under the Marshall Plan by all western European nations but rejected by the USSR and its allies. The biggest amount – $2,825 million – went to Britain, with France receiving $2,445 million. Italy, the western half of Germany, and Austria, all Axis allies during the war, also received large amounts. The aid restored the European economy and tied Western Europe, economically and politically, to the USA. Because the USSR refused to accept aid, the plan confirmed the post-war division of Europe into west and east.

> **Our policy is directed not against any country but against hunger, poverty, desperation and chaos.**

US Secretary of State George Marshall proposes aid to war-torn Europe, June 1947

Counting the Dead

No one knows how many people died during the war, but the total was at least 55 million people killed in battle or on the home front on both sides of the conflict. The worst affected countries were the USSR, which suffered more than 20 million deaths, and Poland, which lost one-fifth of its population. The total death toll included more than 6 million Jews killed in the Holocaust.

The Economic Cost

The economic cost of the war was also immense. At the end of the war, food production in Europe was halved and industrial production was down to one-third of pre-war levels. France lost almost half its pre-war wealth, Italy one-third, while the central areas of almost all large British, German, Italian, Japanese and Polish cities had been destroyed or seriously damaged.

The war also created millions of refugees who had been thrown out of their homes by invading armies or had fled the conflict for their safety. Hundreds of thousands of Germans poured west in the last months of the war in fear of the invading Red Army, hoping for better treatment under the western Allies.

War Crimes

The victorious Allies decided that leading Nazi and Japanese officials should stand trial accused of various war crimes. At Nuremberg in Germany, the

Across Europe many towns and cities were almost completely destroyed in air raids.

International Military Tribunal of US, British, French and Soviet judges tried 21 leading Nazis, 11 of whom were sentenced to death. In Japan, seven wartime leaders, including General Tojo, prime minister during the war, were hanged, while 16 others were sentenced to life imprisonment. Trials of less important officials continued for many years.

Economic Reconstruction

At first the war-ravaged countries were left to rebuild themselves, but once it proved impossible for them to do so, the USA stepped in. The US economy had thrived during the war, as it had not been bombed or invaded. In 1947 George Marshall, US Secretary of State, proposed a "European Recovery Program" – known as the Marshall Plan – to help European nations rebuild their shattered economies. More than $13,700 million – about $130,000 million today – was given by the time aid ended in 1952.

1945-1960

November 1945-September 1946 Main war crimes trial held at Nuremberg; 12 other trials of 156 less-important German and Austrian war criminals end the next year.

5 June 1947 George Marshall proposes European Recovery Program at a speech at Harvard University.

July 1947 Western European nations meet in Paris, France, to discuss the administration of Marshall aid.

April 1948 Organisation of European Economic Cooperation (OEEC) set up in Paris to support economic development of Western Europe.

December War crimes trials end in Tokyo.

December 1953 George Marshall awarded Nobel Prize for Peace for his work to reconstruct Europe after the war.

December 1960 OEEC becomes the international Organisation for Economic Cooperation and Development (OECD), today one of the world's most important economic organisations.

A Divided World

The end of the war was meant to bring peace to the world, but instead it began a period of division between east and west that became known as the Cold War. This lasted for over 40 years.

The United Nations

The United Nations was born on 1 January 1942, when President Roosevelt and Prime Minister Winston Churchill met for the first time since the USA had joined the war. They issued the *Declaration of the United Nations* (that is, those allies fighting Germany, Italy and Japan), calling for a "more permanent system of security". On 26 June 1945, leaders of 50 Allied nations met in San Francisco to sign the UN Charter.

The charter set out three aims: to maintain peace and security, develop friendly relations between states, and encourage countries to work together to solve outstanding issues. Today almost every country in the world is a member of the UN. UN-sanctioned troops keep the peace on many continents.

Two Systems

The two main victors of the war were the USA and USSR, as both Britain and France were economically exhausted by the war. The USA wanted to rebuild European nations as capitalist democracies, but the USSR wanted to establish a series of communist nations in Eastern Europe that would protect it from attack again.

The two superpowers, along with Britain and France, divided Germany, its capital Berlin, and Austria between them. Within four years, the USSR had set up communist governments in East Germany and across Eastern Europe. The USA used Marshall Aid to support the capitalist nations of Western Europe. By 1949 Europe was divided into two armed camps.

The Cold War

The rivalry between the two superpowers soon turned into a 40-year "cold war" of ideas and propaganda. Although the two did not fight each other, they came close to war over Berlin, where a wall was built to separate the communist east and capitalist west. Their allies fought wars in Korea, Vietnam and across Africa. Both sides built up stocks of nuclear weapons, and in 1961 brought the world close to nuclear war in a dispute over Soviet missiles on the island of Cuba.

The End of the War

The end of the Cold War came in the 1980s. In 1985 a new Soviet leader, Mikhail Gorbachev, came to power and began to reform his country. The reforms, however, weakened the USSR and led to the withdrawal of its troops from Eastern Europe. In 1989 communist regimes fell from power across the region, the Berlin Wall was demolished and in 1990 Germany itself was reunited. The following year, the USSR itself collapsed.

The European Union

Two important international organisations grew out of World War Two: the United Nations (see box) and the European Union. After 1945 leading politicians in France and Germany decided to work together. In 1957 they set up the European Economic Community (EEC) along with Italy, Belgium, Luxembourg and the Netherlands. By May 2004 the EEC had become the European Union, with 25 member nations. After centuries of warfare and division Europe had been politically and economically united.

East German troops guard the Berlin Wall in the 1960s.

1945-2004

February 1945 US, Soviet and British leaders meeting in Yalta, Crimea, agree four-power division with France of Germany, Berlin and Austria.

June 1945 UN Charter signed in San Francisco, USA.

July 1945 British Prime Minister Winston Churchill loses power in general election to Labour Party led by Clement Attlee.

March 1946 Winston Churchill describes an "Iron Curtain" dividing Europe in two, during a speech in Fulton, Missouri, USA.

September 1946-February 1948 Communist regimes set up in Bulgaria, Romania, Poland, Hungary and Czechoslovakia.

April 1949 USA, Canada and nine European nations set up North Atlantic Treaty Organisation (NATO) to defend themselves against Soviet attack.

May 1949 US, French and British occupation zones combine to form West Germany.

October 1949 Soviet occupation zone becomes East Germany.

May 1955 USSR and seven eastern European communist nations establish Warsaw Pact defence organisation.

May 1955 Austria reunited as a neutral nation as occupying troops withdrawn.

March 1957 Treaty of Rome sets up the six-nation European Economic Community.

August 1961 East Germans erect Berlin Wall to divide city between communist east and capitalist west.

December 1988 USSR begins to withdraw troops from Eastern Europe, leading to overthrow of communism and democratic elections throughout region.

November 1989 Berlin Wall comes down.

October 1990 West and East Germany unite.

December 1991 USSR collapses and is replaced by 15 independent states, including Russia, ending the Cold War.

May 2004 European Union expands to 25 members.

Maps

Axis expansion in Europe by 1942

Allied countries	*Greater Germany*	*German-occupied territory*	*Italy and Italian-occupied territory*	*Countries under Axis control*	*Neutral countries*

Japanese conquests in the Pacific up to March 1942

U S S R

MONGOLIA

Manchuria

CHINA

KOREA

JAPAN

Tokyo

Line of maximum Japanese expansion, March 1942

Pacific Ocean

OKINAWA

IWO JIMA

MIDWAY

HAWAIIAN ISLANDS

Pearl Harbor

BURMA

Hong Kong

PHILIPPINE ISLANDS

MARIANAS

THAILAND

FRENCH INDO-CHINA

Manila

Philippine Sea

MARSHALL ISLANDS

MALAYA

Singapore

SARAWAK

SUMATRA

BORNEO

DUTCH NEW GUINEA

NEW GUINEA

SOLOMON ISLANDS

JAVA

DUTCH EAST INDIES

Port Moresby

GUADALCANAL

Coral Sea

NEW CALEDONIA

AUSTRALIA

NEW ZEALAND

Glossary

Ally A country linked with another by treaty or friendship.

Anti-Semitism Prejudice against Jewish people.

Armed services The military forces of a nation, usually the army, air force and navy.

Armistice An agreement between opposing sides to cease firing weapons while a peace agreement is agreed.

Beachhead A landing place on an enemy beach.

Blitzkrieg A German term meaning "lightning war", originally applied to a rapid attack by tanks and other armoured vehicles; the British later applied the term to describe air attacks on London and other cities and shortened it to "the Blitz".

Capitalism An economic system based on the private ownership of industry, finance and property.

Civilian A person whose main job is not connected to the military.

Coalition An alliance between different political parties in a government.

Colony A region or country controlled by another country as part of an empire.

Communism Belief in a society that exists without different social classes, in which everyone is equal and all property is owned by the people.

Convoy A fleet of merchant ships escorted by armed warships in order to protect them.

Democracy Government by the people or their elected representatives, often forming opposing political parties.

Dictator A leader who takes complete control of a country and often rules by force.

Empire A group of different nations and peoples, ruled by one nation and its emperor.

Fascism An extreme political movement based on nationalism (extreme loyalty to one's country) and authority, often military, which aims to unite a country's people into a disciplined force under an all-powerful leader.

Führer German word for "leader", a title taken by Hitler after 1934.

Holocaust The attempt by the Nazis to murder all the Jews in Europe.

League of Nations An organisation set up in 1919, after World War One, which tried to solve disputes between countries.

Nationalist A person who is passionately loyal and devoted to his or her own country.

Nazi Party The National Socialist Party of Adolf Hitler, with extreme fascist beliefs, that ruled Germany from 1933-45.

Neutral A nation that refuses to take sides in a war and does not fight.

Partisan A member of an armed resistance group fighting inside a country against an invading or occupying army.

Rationing A fixed allowance of food, provisions, fuel and so on, especially in time of scarcity, such as war, set by the government.

Red Army The army of the USSR.

Reich The German word for "empire"; Hitler's Germany was often called the Third Reich, as it followed two previous German empires.

Republic A country governed by an elected head of state called a president.

Strategic Of great geographic, military or economic importance.

Superpower A country with an overwhelming military and economic power, such as the USA or USSR.

Total war A war involving every aspect of a country's military, economic, industrial and human resources.

Treaty A formal agreement between two or more countries.

USSR The Union of the Soviet Socialist Republics, or the Soviet Union, which existed from 1922-91; commonly known as Russia.

WEBSITES

www.spartacus.schoolnet.co.uk/2WW.htm
A comprehensive site covering every aspect of World War Two, including both the military campaign and the home front.

www.bbc.co.uk/history/war/wwtwo/index.shtml
The official BBC site on the war, with numerous photographs, maps, and spoken word extracts.

www.historyplace.com/worldwar2/timeline/ww2time.htm
A detailed timeline of events from 1918 to the end of World War Two, with many photos.

Index